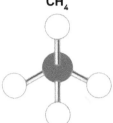

Methane Gas
Chemical Formula:
CH_4

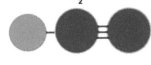

Nitrous Oxide Gas
Chemical Formula:
N_2O

Ozone Ga
Chemical For
O_3

MW00615258

Good Morning Trees

Remember to
enjoy and
protect our
Earth!
- Aisha Nnoli

WRITTEN AND ILLUSTRATED BY
Aisha Nnoli

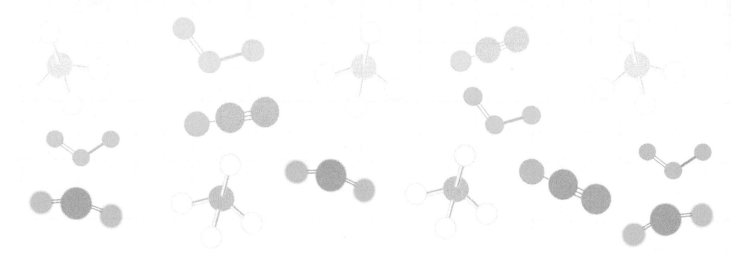

Special thank you to educational consultant Dr. James Borneman. You inspired me through your classes and research mentorship at UC Riverside.

Copyright © 2021 Aisha Nnoli
All rights reserved.

No part of this publication may be reproduced in whole or in part, or stored in a retrieval system, or transmitted in any form or by any means, electronic, mechanical, photocopying, recording, or otherwise, without written permission from the publisher. For information regarding permission, write to Aisha Nnoli.

Published in University Place, Washington.

Library of Congress Control Number: 2021902801
ISBN: 978-0-578-85688-9

To my mother, Gladys, who encourages everyone to remain curious.

When daylight breaks and the
morning has begun,
trees can be seen shimmering in
the sun.

Plants grow from tiny seeds to big majestic trees,
by converting carbon dioxide from the air into carbon we can see.

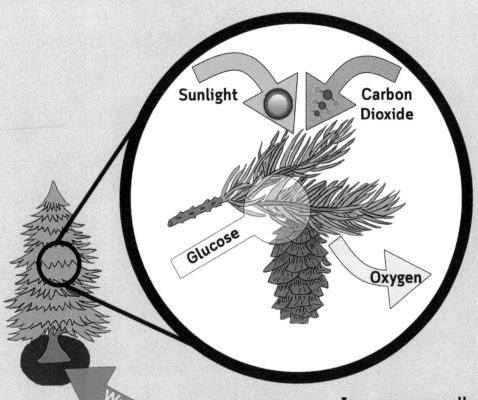

In a process called photosynthesis, plants use energy from sunlight to change water and carbon dioxide into glucose (a type of sugar plants use for food) and oxygen (a gas most animals need for survival).

Carbon dioxide (CO_2) comes from many sources, either natural or from humans burning fuels.
An example is the CO_2 produced while driving to and from our schools.

Carbon dioxide
(CO_2)

Up into the atmosphere this
colorless gas will go,
accumulating with car emissions
from others who drove.

To understand why we should
care about this gas,
we need to explain a greenhouse
and its glass.

**Visible sunlight passes through the
clear glass walls,
heating objects big and small.**

The heat released from objects inside,
is trapped inside by the glass and
begins its ride.
Around and around the heat will grow,
warmer inside as molecules move to
and fro.

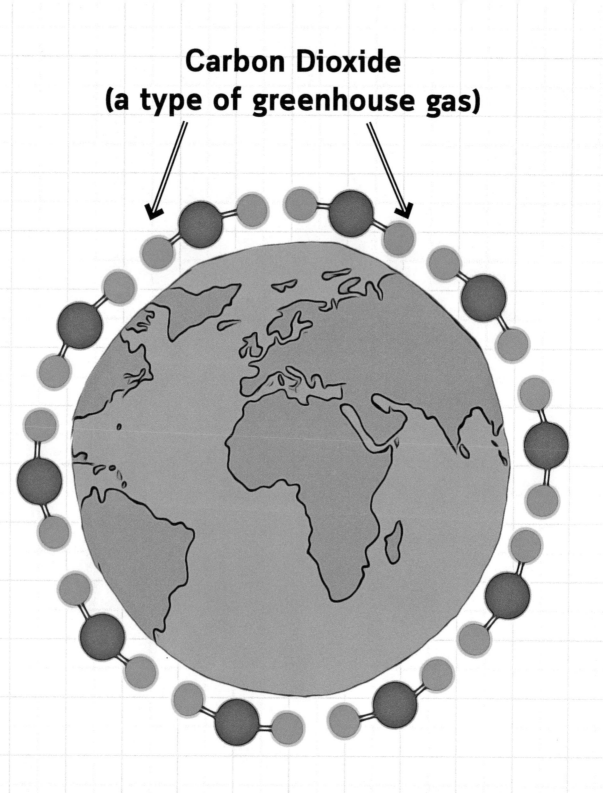

Carbon Dioxide
(a type of greenhouse gas)

Now imagine if carbon dioxide were to replace the glass, surrounding Earth in a greenhouse gas.

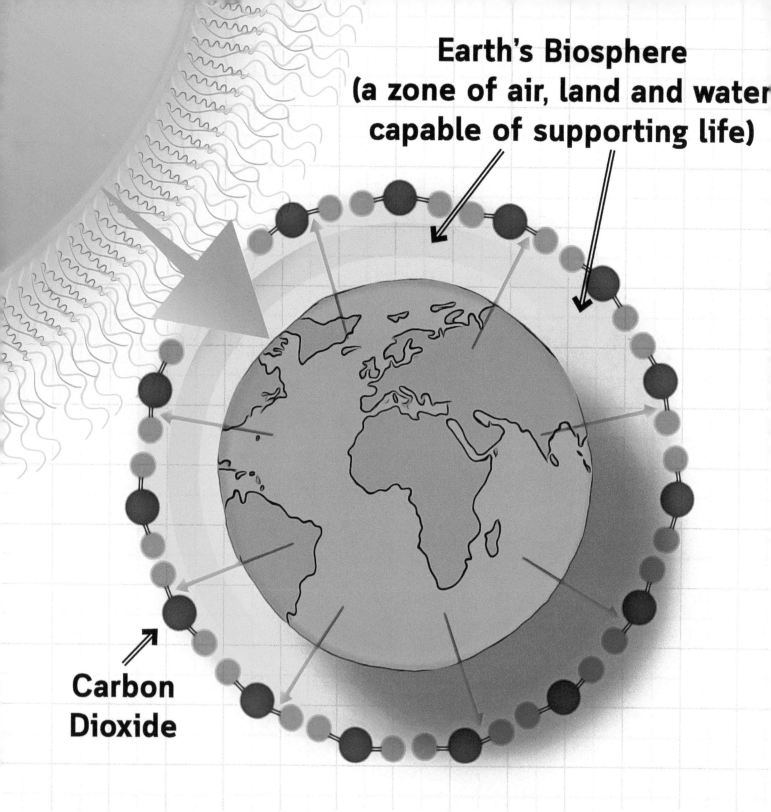

**Earth's Biosphere
(a zone of air, land and water
capable of supporting life)**

**Carbon
Dioxide**

**When sunlight shines through the Earth's atmosphere,
heat is reflected back into our biosphere.**

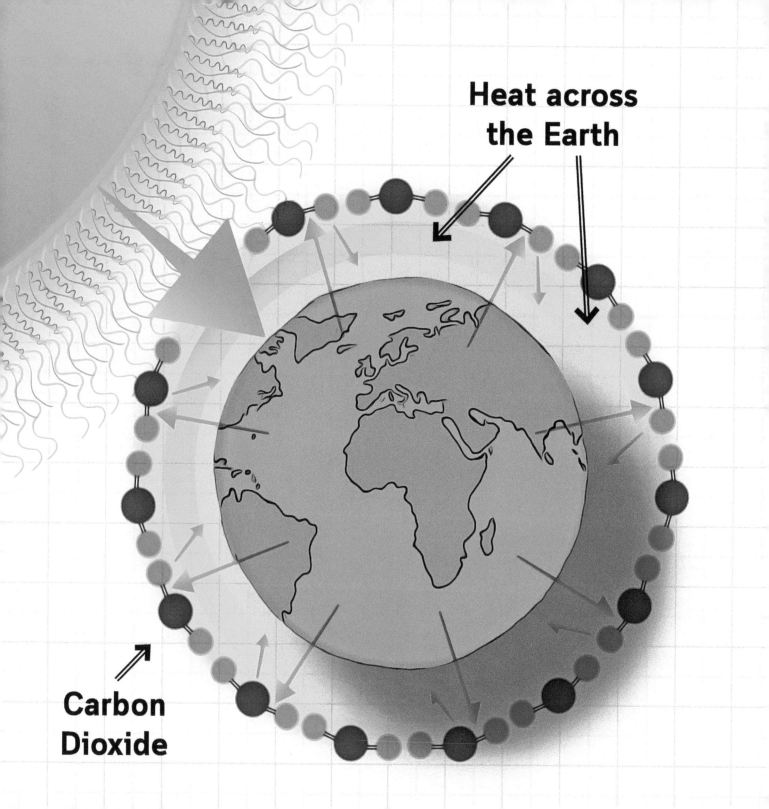

Heat across
the Earth

Carbon
Dioxide

Carbon dioxide traps some of this heat across the globe, preventing Earth from becoming too cold.

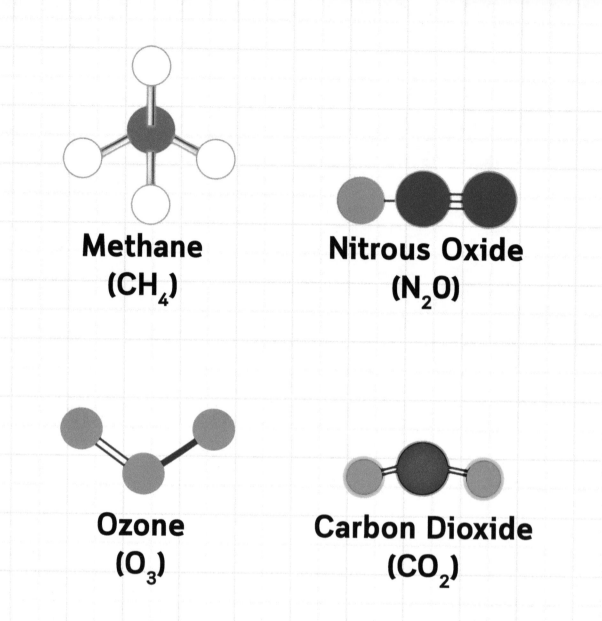

Methane (CH$_4$)

Nitrous Oxide (N$_2$O)

Ozone (O$_3$)

Carbon Dioxide (CO$_2$)

Types of Greenhouse Gases

To keep our Earth warm, methane, nitrous oxide and ozone act similar to carbon dioxide when in gas form.

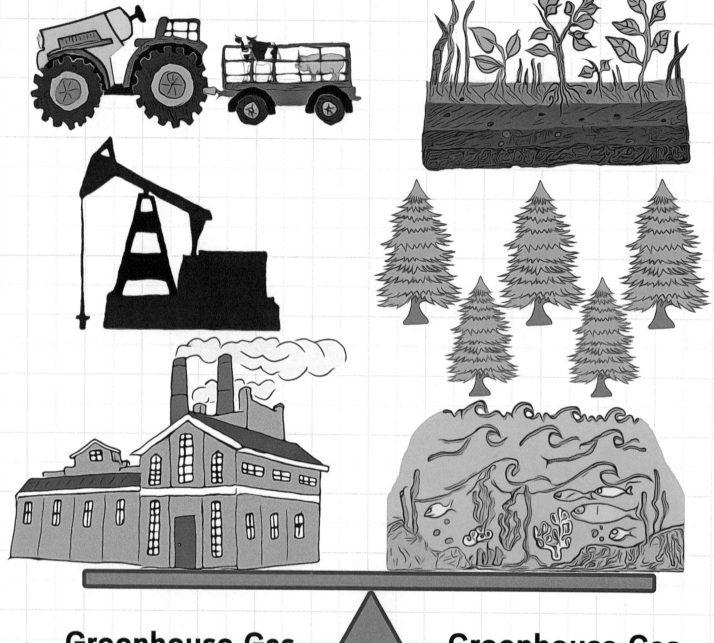

Greenhouse Gas Sources   **Greenhouse Gas Sinks**

Greenhouse gases are not a big deal, when the balance between their sources and sinks are ideal.

Sources release greenhouse gases into our atmosphere.

Sinks remove greenhouse gases from our atmosphere.

Examples of greenhouse gas sources are industry, agriculture, and fossil fuel use,
while sinks include the ocean, soil and plants such as the red spruce.

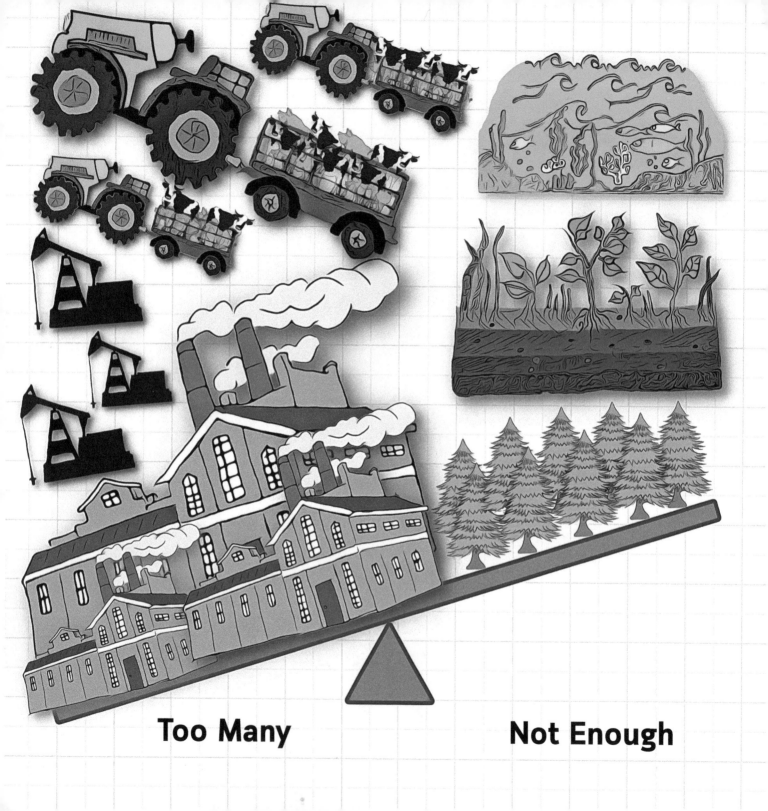

Too Many

Not Enough

**Unfortunately,
balance is no longer the case,
as greenhouse sources are greater
than sinks can erase.**

Heatwaves and droughts

Flood, storms, and hurricanes

Dying coral reefs and fish

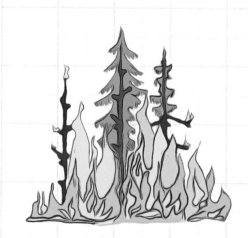

Wildfires

Melting glaciers and rising sea levels

Air pollution

The increase in greenhouse sources is causing the temperature of our Earth to slowly rise. This process is called global warming and to ignore it would be unwise.

Thankfully, mitigation and adaptation are things we can do...

to prevent efforts against global warming from falling through.

Planting

Carpooling

**Alternative
Transportation**

Conserve Energy

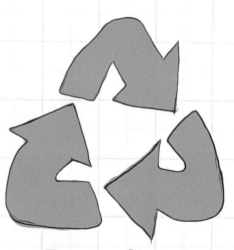

Recycling

Mitigation involves actions in which greenhouse sources are reduced and greenhouse sinks are given a boost.

Build Floodways

Water Conservation

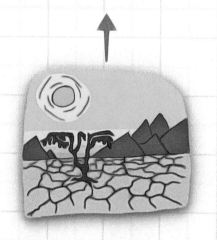

Preparing for and preventing wildfires

We need to change the way we see and use our Earth.

Coral nurseries and Sustainable fishing

Education and Strengthening ecosystems

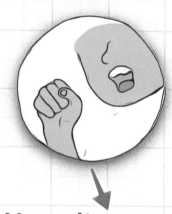

Air quality governance and Weatherization

Adaptation is when we adjust to current climate changes, and prepare for increases in future global temperature ranges.

**Each of us must do our part to reduce the greenhouse gases,
our efforts need to be collective and sustainable as time passes.**

Trees are a reminder of how important balance is in nature, their beauty can inspire us to protect the Earth alongside our neighbors.

CPSIA information can be obtained
at www.ICGtesting.com
Printed in the USA
BVHW061502240921
617464BV00002B/13